THREE-YEAR
ALLOTMENT
NOTEBOOK

Frances Lincoln Limited
4 Torriano Mews
Torriano Avenue
London NW5 2RZ
www.franceslincoln.com

A catalogue record for this book is available
from the British Library

Please note that the planting guidelines
included throughout are suggestions only
and adjustments will have to be made
according to location.

ISBN 978-0-7112-3155-9

9 8 7 6 5 4 3 2 1

First Frances Lincoln edition 2010

ACKNOWLEDGMENTS
This notebook would not exist if it wasn't for Fulham
Palace Meadows Allotments and for the many other
allotments we were fortunate enough to visit and
walk around. We are very grateful indeed to all the
plotholders we met, for their generosity and their
willingness to share. In particular we would like to
thank Caroline Abraham, Mrs Afsardayr, Mr and Mrs
Armand Attard, John Baker, John Bartell, Michael
Freude, Jane and Pedro Garcia, Mr and Mrs Milorad
Gajic, Rob Geeson, Tony Hannaford, Jack Hudson,
Maria Knight, Gillian Moss, Oliver Murray, Karl
Openshaw, John Schoen, Stefan Sherwood, Philip
Smith, Gillian Traverso.

We are very grateful to Julian Ashby, Julia Brown,
Brian Clayton, Martin Colyer, Bob Flowerdew, Hugo
Greer-Walker, Paul Huxley, Veronica Pratt, Adam
Robertson, Eddie Robinson, Sarah Sands, Cleve
West and Christine Eatwell, Alan Withers and
Christopher Woodward who all supported the book
in some way. Also, grateful thanks to Gwyn Headley,
Yvonne Seeley and Jacqui Norman of Fotolibra for
their unfailing helpfulness.

A big thank you to our publishers, Frances Lincoln
Publishers Ltd; to our editor, Anna Sanderson and
designer, Maria Charalambous.

THREE-YEAR ALLOTMENT
NOTEBOOK
Joanna Cruddas
PHOTOGRAPHY BY Edwina Sassoon

INTRODUCTION

'What makes you think you'll have time for an allotment?' my local Allotments' Chairman asked one day when I was nagging him about the long waiting list. 'I'll manage,' I said. But with a full-time job, I felt the full weight of his 'an allotment isn't just for Christmas' warning. My dream was to grow rows of cutting flowers. As a sideline there would be vegetables.

It was a baking hot July morning when the call came to say a plot was available. A few days later I was standing by a parched, oblong patch of earth. Back at the allotments' office I read the Association's terms and conditions. Fifty per cent of a plot had to be cultivated for vegetables. 'Fifty per cent vegetables?', I queried casually. 'You know about vegetable growing?' the Secretary asked. 'Crop rotation, all that …' Before I could answer he continued, 'Don't worry, people will help. There isn't an inspection until the end of September.' Inspection … I felt like the new girl at school as I wove my way back to what was now my plot, hidden somewhere in the maze of 400 others.

Almost immediately a neighbour strolled over. 'Here, have these.' My first allotment friend, Teri, held out a handful of bean seeds. Later, as I was leaving, a hand clutched my arm. 'You're new, aren't you? Come.' I followed Lena to her plot where a row of sweet peas was in full flower. 'Pick as many as you like,' she said and disappeared. That day was the beginning of many new friendships. It was also the day I turned my back on perfectly formed, bought vegetables and converted to the pleasure and value of grow-your-own; to the benefits of eating seasonal vegetables, plot-to-pot within the hour.

Back at my plot, I realized a solid piece of earth needs dividing into sections and walkways would be helpful; my plot needed to be given shape. I started with very few tools, later importing an old wooden chest to store them in. From the start, my gardening friend and photographer Edwina Sassoon suggested she would visually record progress while I sketched plans, made notes of plantings, successes and disappointments. We started visiting other allotment sites in cities and in the heart of the countryside, finding enthusiasm, expertise and a willingness to share knowledge wherever we went.

Most allotmenteers have limited time – often just 2 or 3 hours a week – to achieve maximum reward. Joining in the chat around the water pump, I found newcomers wanted bullet-point information to reach this goal: when to plant what; tips to keep the plot in control and the inspection committee sweet.

I find keeping notes throughout the year simplifies the following one. Starting each year with a plan keeps the veg in some order. It is interesting to compare planting and harvesting dates from year to year. The intention of this *Three-Year Allotment Notebook* is to combine a quick reference guide with journal pages in which to record personal experiences. Allowing for different climates, and to encourage successional sowing and therefore a long harvest, there is some repetition and overlap of sowing and planting through the months. We have tried to include as many options as possible. 'Keeping the Plot' tasks are also duplicated if there are several months when something can be done. At the back of the book there is graph paper so you can plan planting and crop rotation (there is a suggested three-year-cycle rotation) each year, plus a place for notes and recording contacts and suppliers.

Between months we have included sections suggesting different ways you might look after your plot – whether by nurturing the soil, planning planting, putting up a shed or creating a space to relax in – and through Edwina's photographs we have tried to show a variety of ideas for creating a successful and imaginative plot and to share the beauty of allotment sites around the year.

Joanna Cruddas

JANUARY

January is the month to plan your plot. Draw a scaled diagram on the graph paper at the end of this book and plan your space. Regular crop rotation (grouping vegetables according to their families – alliums, brassicas, legumes, potatoes and roots – and rotating where you plant them) helps keep vegetables disease free (see Crop Rotation). Order your seeds for the year, remembering you have limited space! Start saving egg boxes for chitting seed potatoes in February. Harvest remaining root vegetables this month and next.

The January allotment, bare of vegetation, may look uninviting but it presents a great opportunity to see your plot with fresh eyes. Now is the time to make any changes to planting locations and consider improvements such as creating seating, storage or wildlife-friendly areas.

KEEPING THE PLOT

Check your shed or storage chest, if you have one. Tidy and ensure it is weatherproof and secure.
Finish digging and spreading soil improver in preparation for the spring
Mulch around spring cabbages
Order seed potatoes
Repair paths around your plot
Stake Brussels sprouts to protect them from wind

SOWING & PLANTING

Sow indoors, or outside under cover, if your climate is very mild. Preferably start in a greenhouse or on window ledges for planting out in March.
Legumes Broad beans, sugar snap peas
Rhubarb Plant out new sets; divide old crowns and start forcing
Roots radishes
Salad and leaves Lettuces, spinach (sown outdoors under cover)

JANUARY

JANUARY

JANUARY

PLANNING A PLOT

Planning your plot is a compromise between your dreams, accommodating your allotments' regulations and the site of the plot you have inherited. Consider your priorities: storage, a place to relax, positioning your compost heap and conserving water. There are plenty of ideas throughout this notebook.

(Below) Walkways create order on your plot and prevent the soil from getting compacted. Logs or pavings can be used as stepping stones. Wood chippings make good pathways and are quick and easy to lay. Look at the photographs throughout this book for ideas on different materials and methods for creating walkways and raised beds.

Raised beds (above) provide a concentrated area of fertile soil for intensive planting.

(Above) You will need stakes for supporting climbing plants such as runner and other climbing beans or sweet peas. Horizontal bracing will give the stakes – and the plants – additional support as well.

Depending on your allotments' regulations, your plot may need numbering. In which case, ensure your sign is visible, legible and firmly mounted or anchored in the ground.

Two rows of wood tracking (below) or planks laid a few inches apart divide a plot and provide walkways, and the narrow space between can be planted up with bulbs or small plants.

FEBRUARY

If you haven't already cleared and fed your plot, be sure to do so by the end of the month, so that any added organic matter has time to break down before you start sowing and planting out. Fleece tunnel cloches (see below) protect young plants from frost. Chit early potatoes on a cool window ledge.

(Right) The raspberry canes shown here will be cut down to the ground in February/March.

(Bottom, right) Freshly-dug drills in preparation for planting potatoes.

KEEPING THE PLOT

Beware Slugs and snails become active with the warmer weather
Birds are hungry. Check that brassicas, onion sets and seed beds particularly are well netted.
Complete all digging
Cover rhubarb and divide crowns if compacted
Feed asparagus plants with general fertilizer
Prepare new asparagus beds
Prune autumn raspberries

SOWING

Sow indoors, or outside if your climate is very mild and you can provide shelter:
Brassicas Autumn cabbage, kales
Leeks, spring onions, cucumbers, peppers, tomatoes and aubergines should be sown indoors. A warm window ledge is ideal.
Legumes Broad beans, peas
Roots radishes
Salad and leaves Lettuce, rocket, spinach

PLANTING OUT

If mild, plant out:
Alliums Garlic, onion and shallot sets
Legumes Broad beans (sown in autumn)
Rhubarb sets
Roots Jerusalem artichokes

FEBRUARY

FEBRUARY

FEBRUARY

MARCH

Be wary of being lulled into a false sense of security with occasional warm days in March. Fork over the whole plot and sow green manure such as phacelia (see October/Nurturing Your Soil) in areas saved for summer planting. Soil should be moist but not cold to touch for sowing or planting out. Covering the ground with fleece or plastic warms it up and also keeps weeds at bay. Chit early and maincrop potatoes on a cool window ledge.

(Below) Plastic bottles, with the base removed, make good individual greenhouses for protecting tender seedlings.

(Opposite, top) Net young plants to protect from birds.

(Opposite, below) Set up string guides to ensure straight sowing and to mark the location of seeds.

SOWING INDOORS

Aubergine, celeriac, chillies, cucumbers, globe artichokes, peppers, tomatoes should all be sown indoors for planting out later

SOWING OUTDOORS

Alliums Leeks, onion sets, spring onions
Brassicas Cabbages, calabrese, kohl rabi
Legumes Broad beans and peas
Roots and potatoes Beetroots, carrots, parsnips, turnips
Salad and leaves Lettuces, rocket, spinach, Swiss chard

PLANTING OUT

Alliums Garlic, onion and shallot sets
Asparagus crowns
Brassicas Cauliflowers
Fruit Blackberries, currants, raspberries, strawberries
Legumes Broad beans, peas
Roots and potatoes Early potatoes, Jerusalem artichokes

KEEPING THE PLOT

Feed any crops that have wintered in the ground such as brassicas and salad leaves
Net all fruit bushes
Prepare a frame for climbing plants
Prune and feed autumn raspberries, mature blueberries, currants, gooseberries
Rake seedbeds before sowing seeds; sprinkle with fertilizer
Remove cloches from rhubarb
Trim and tidy plot edges
Weed regularly

MARCH

MARCH

MARCH

SHEDS

A plotholder's shed is his castle. Planning its site and surround is important. Check for any allotment restrictions for building a hut, particularly with regard to height and size. Will it create shade for you or your neighbour and will this be welcome? Consider building it from recycled materials and using the roof as guttering to supply water to a water butt.

A low or sunken hut provides storage and is a clever solution to any height restrictions. It is also ideal for creating a sedum roof (see opposite). Solar panels may provide energy to pump water or boil a kettle (see opposite, bottom left). Painting your shed not only prolongs its life but allows your imagination to have free rein ...

APRIL

Seedlings, started off indoors, may be ready to be planted out by the end of the month, but harden off first and don't plant out tender plants until the danger of frost is passed. An easy alternative to seeds are plug plants, which are widely available. Select and order or buy your annual flower seeds for sowing in trays indoors or straight into the ground in May.

(Below) Earth up potatoes as foliage pushes through the soil.

SOWING INDOORS

Aubergines, sweetcorn, celeriac, courgettes, cucumbers, Florence fennel, French beans, kale, pumpkins, squash, runner beans, tomatoes

KEEPING THE PLOT

Earth up sprouting potatoes
Feed currant bushes, blueberries and strawberry plants unless you fed in March
Protect small plants from birds and vermin
Remove rhubarb cloches if you haven't already done so
Sow small quantities of salad leaves every three weeks for successional harvesting
Sow sweet peas in growing position beside stakes to allow them to climb
Stake and support peas and broad beans (see opposite)
Start a herb bed
Weed regularly

SOWING OUTDOORS

Alliums Leeks, onion sets, spring onions
Brassicas Brussels sprouts, cabbages, calabrese, cauliflowers, kohl rabi, sprouting broccoli
Legumes Broad beans and peas
Roots Beetroot, parsnips, turnips, radishes
Salad and leaves Lettuces, oriental leaves, spinach, Swiss chard

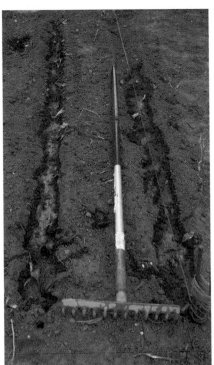

PLANTING OUT

Alliums Garlic, onion and shallot sets
Asparagus crowns need to be planted by the end of April
Brassicas Kale, kohl rabi, sprouting broccoli
Fruit Strawberries
Legumes Broad beans, peas
Potatoes and roots Globe artichokes, Jerusalem artichokes, potatoes (last earlies and maincrop)
Salad and leaves Lettuces, oriental leaves, radishes

APRIL

APRIL

APRIL

TOOLS

A sturdy fork, spade, trowel and watering can make a starter kit. Next, you will want secateurs, string, knife, padlock and a strong pair of gloves. A rake, hoe and dibber are near essentials. Shears or a strimmer may be needed to trim grass paths and if your allotments don't supply communal wheelbarrows, you will need your own. The ideal plot has a shed for storage, but there are other more modest options such as a strong chest which can double as a seat.

(Left) Optimize space by wedging small, sharp tools in a door- or shed-frame for safety and visibility. Alternatively, knock in a few nails and hang up with string.

(Opposite, above) Gumboots are best stored upside down.

(Opposite, bottom left) An up-ended pallet can contain tools and divide the plot; however, tools will be exposed to the elements and vulnerable to theft.

(Opposite, bottom right) A chest can be locked and doubles as seat and storage, but small items slip to the bottom so consider internal organization ideas such as containers with lids.

MAY

Leave yourself space to relax and admire your plot during the summer (see July/Seating). When sowing or planting out, bear in mind the eventual size of the plant the seed will produce. Space for good ventilation around your vegetables helps prevent disease. Regular watering helps prevent mildew. Remember to protect tender seedlings against an unexpected cold spell.

Borage and nasturtiums scattered between vegetables are decorative and provide flowers for cutting and eating. Nigella may deter carrot fly. Sow or plant easy-to-grow annuals for cutting throughout the summer such as asters, cornflowers, cosmos, dahlias, nigella, sunflowers, sweet peas and zinnias. Look out for elderflowers around your allotments for making elderflower cordial.

(Right) Bamboo or hazel sticks make good supports for climbing beans and sweet peas.

(Left) Use newspaper to make biodegradable pots. Unwrap or plant straight into the ground, where the paper will decompose.

PLANTING OUT

Artichoke, celery, Florence fennel, leek, sweetcorn can all be planted out
Aubergines, chillies, peppers, courgettes, cucumbers, pumpkins, squashes, runner and French beans, tomatoes can be planted out towards the end of the month when all danger of frost has passed
Brassicas If you started these off indoors, or have bought plants, they can now be planted out. Give them space to grow!
Potatoes Maincrops should be planted by the end May

KEEPING THE PLOT

Create a wigwam for climbing beans
Earth up potatoes
Hoe frequently to keep weeds down
Mulch fruit crops to keep the soil moist
Net soft fruits
Pinch out broad bean and pea tips once pods start to form; stake well
Pull out raspberry suckers
Remove strawberry runners; put straw or paper under fruit for protection
Start removing side shoots from early tomatoes
Stop pulling rhubarb at the end of May to ensure next year's harvest
Thin carrots, beetroot, Florence fennel while still small
Water if dry

SOWING OUTDOORS

Brassicas These all need space and are slow growing: cabbage, calabrese, cauliflower, kale, kohl rabi, purple-sprouting broccoli
Courgettes, cucumbers, pumpkins and squashes Wait until well into the month and the soil is warm through
Herbs Sow basil, coriander and parsley every few weeks for a constant supply through the summer
Legumes French and runner beans. peas, mangetouts, sugar snap peas
Roots Beetroot, carrots, Florence fennel, swedes, turnips, radishes
Salad and leaves Lettuces, oriental leaves, rocket
Sweetcorn Sow in blocks for successful pollination

MAY

MAY

MAY

CREATIVE PLANTING

Your plot is your front and back garden, permanently on show to your neighbours. You can decorate your hut with climbers or a window box, or by growing strawberries in vertical wall planters. A pergola, covered by a vine or hybrid berries, will create shade and privacy (see July/Seating). Intersperse flowers with vegetables to encourage pollination, discourage aphids, optimize use of space and provide some welcome colour.

(This page) Growing marigolds among vegetables helps deter aphids and adds colour.

(Below, right) Mixed plantings of rudbeckia, marigolds and ruby chard create a feast of colour.

(Opposite page, left) Tall sunflowers around a greenhouse offer welcome shade.

(Opposite page, right) Grow morning glory up climbing beans for late summer colour.

JUNE

Plant out any seedlings you've been nurturing indoors. Optimize use of your space by sowing quick-growing crops such as radishes or salad leaves in temporarily unoccupied ground or between slower-growing crops. Under-sow tall sunflowers with dwarf ones. Red and green lettuces will decorate your plot and your plate (see opposite).

Runner beans can grow to 8ft (2.4m). Supporting stakes need to be tall enough (see below).

PLANTING OUT

Alliums Leeks
Aubergines, chillies, sweet peppers and tomatoes
Brassicas Broccoli, Brussels sprouts, cabbages, cauliflowers, kale
Fruit Strawberries
Legumes French and runner beans
Roots and bulbs Artichokes, celery, celerlac
Salad and leaves Endives, radicchio
Squashes etc Courgettes, pumpkins, squashes, cucumbers
Sweetcorn Plant out in blocks

KEEPING THE PLOT

Earth up potatoes
Feed blueberries
Hoe weeds regularly
Look out for asparagus beetle and pick off by hand
Net brassicas and all fruit
Pinch out broad bean tips and side shoots from tomatoes
Prune mildew out of gooseberries
Remove raspberry suckers
Stake French and runner beans. Support peas with peasticks or wire netting
Stake and cross-string broad beans for support
Stop cutting asparagus by the end of June; then feed with general fertilizer
Tie in sweet peas and check they are well supported
Thin root crop seedlings
Trim path edges to keep couch grass and weeds off the plot
Water regularly and thoroughly

SOWING OUTDOORS

Brassicas Broccoli, kale, kohl rabi
Legumes French beans, peas, runner beans
Roots and bulbs Beetroot, carrots, Florence fennel, swedes, turnips
Salad and leaves Lettuce, oriental leaves, Swiss chard
Squashes etc Courgettes, cucumbers, pumpkins, squashes

JUNE

JUNE

JUNE

WATERING

Summer watering is one of the most important aspects of allotment life. Before taking on your plot, locate the nearest water supply. Is it a hand pump (see opposite, bottom left) or is there the luxury of running water? Make the most of rainwater by putting up guttering with a downpipe to a butt (see opposite, top). Not only will this supply a significant amount of rainwater but it will be close to hand. Leaving out buckets to collect rainwater will also save you having to carry it any distance.

Watering in the evening or very early morning avoids evaporation. It is better to water less often but for longer, as soaking the ground thoroughly encourages roots to grow more deeply.

Give discarded water tanks and cisterns a new lease of life collecting rain throughout the year.

(Far right) Imaginative recycling creates the perfect container for an unruly hosepipe around a standpipe. The gravel surface underneath maximizes drainage.

JULY

July is the month to enjoy long days in the allotment (see Seating). When planting leeks, create strong-walled holes by using a dibber; drop in the leek seedling and fill the hole with water (see right). Thin carrots in the cool of the evening when they give off less scent, which attracts carrot fly. Ensure all removed carrots and any carrot scraps are buried deep in the compost heap. Keep watering thoroughly and spread mulch on the plot to retain moisture.

Hanging onions and garlic when drying keeps them well ventilated.

KEEPING THE PLOT

Check brassicas for butterfly eggs and asparagus for beetles

Cut back old leaves from strawberry plants, feed them, remove runners and use these to create new plants

Cut out fruited and weak raspberry canes

Draw up soil around the stems of brassicas and sweetcorn to keep them stable

Dry herbs, or pick, chop and freeze them

Earth up potatoes

Feed tomatoes and peppers every ten to fourteen days

Hoe weeds

Lift onions, shallots and garlic and dry in the sun (see August/Harvest)

Pick vegetables while they are young and tender; courgettes can become marrows overnight

Pinch out tomato side shoots throughout the summer

Protect cauliflower heads from the sun by covering with an inverted outside leaf

Spray liquid seaweed solution on bean and pea leaves

Summer prune gooseberries and currants

Watch out for mildew on all plants

SOWING OUTDOORS

Brassicas Cabbages, calabrese, kale, kohl rabi, sprouting broccoli
Legumes Last chance to sow French and runner beans, peas
Roots and bulbs Beetroot, carrots, Florence fennel, turnips, radishes
Salad and leaves Chicory, endive, lettuce, oriental leaves, rocket, salad leaves, Swiss chard

PLANTING OUT

Alliums Leeks
Brassicas Brussels sprouts, cabbages, cauliflowers, kale, sprouting broccoli
Legumes French and runner beans, peas
Roots Beetroot

JULY

JULY

JULY

SEATING

Your relaxation area is an opportunity to create something individual. It can be simple or elaborate. Do you have room for a table – and will you use it? If you anticipate visitors you will need more than one chair ... If your furniture is not weatherproof, is there storage room in your hut? Folding chairs and tables can be hung out of the way on walls or on the back of doors when not in use.

Consider too where to position your seating and ensure it is set apart from compost areas!

Allotment life is sociable and your plot could be the ideal spot for barbecues and picnics. A pergola can provide an outside room for entertainment (opposite, centre bottom). Or you may prefer to enjoy solitary contemplation on a rustic stool (opposite, bottom right) in a shady 'house' created by climbing plants. A bench can double as seating and storage (opposite, top).

AUGUST

August … holidays … and a time to share your produce with friends. If you are going away, arrange a watering and harvest exchange with your fellow plotholders. Pull up finished broad beans, digging their nitrogen-filled roots into the ground. Lift pumpkins and squashes off the ground to prevent rotting – a piece of slate, wood or stone slab will do the trick (see opposite, top).

KEEPING THE PLOT

Check that beans and peas are well supported
Collect seeds from vegetables and flowers
Continue to pinch out tomato side shoots
Cut back lavender; make lavender bags or tied bunches
Deadhead flowers continually to lengthen the growing season
Dry garlic, onions and shallots in the sun before storing
Earth up celery, potatoes
Feed tomatoes and peppers every ten to fourteen days

Hoe weeds
Mulch your plot after watering
Paint or spray woodwork with preserver
Plant out strawberry runners or new plants
Sow green manure in empty spaces
Summer prune fruit bushes – currants, gooseberries, raspberries – after fruiting
Take cuttings from herbs
Tidy paths: cut grass and clip edges
Tie cucumbers, peppers, tomatoes to strong canes
Watch out for slugs and other pests

SOWING OUTDOORS

Brassicas Broccoli, cabbages, kohl rabi
Roots Carrots, radishes
Salad and leaves Lettuces, oriental leaves, rocket, spinach, Swiss chard

PLANTING OUT

Brassicas Cauliflower, kale, broccoli
Fruit Strawberries

AUGUST

AUGUST

AUGUST

HARVEST

Your harvest is your reward – enjoy and admire it. Allotments and glut go hand in hand – as do sharing and exchanging with your plot neighbours. Most fruit and vegetables can be frozen, preserved or dried.

(Opposite, top) Dry French and runner bean seeds and store in jars.

(Left) Cure squashes in the sun before storing in a cool place.

(Near right) Onions also need to be dried in the sun before plaiting and storing. The key to effective drying is good ventilation, so think about raising your produce off the ground in some way. Both the ideas shown here (left and right) are simple and effective and use recycled materials.

SEPTEMBER

It is too early to prepare your plot for the winter, but a good time to record the positioning of the vegetables in order to plan crop rotation for next year (see Crop Rotation). Take a photograph or draw a diagram. Ensure seeds you keep are dry and clean before storing in envelopes or paper bags.

(Left) Carrots grow well in the deep, free-draining soil of raised beds.

(Below, right) Green tomatoes will ripen if left in the sun.

SOWING OUTDOORS

Brassicas Spring cabbage
Roots Carrots, turnips
Salad and leaves
Endives, lettuce, spinach,
Swiss chard

PLANTING OUT

Alliums Onion sets
Brassicas Spring cabbage
Fruit Strawberries

KEEPING THE PLOT

Cut down asparagus fern as
it starts to die; mulch the
bed thoroughly
Cut out old raspberry canes,
tie in new ones
Deadhead flowers to prolong
the growing season
Dry pumpkins and squashes
in the sun before storing;
keep them off the ground
(see Harvest)
Earth up celery
Feed leeks and celeriac with
general fertilizer

Lift remaining onions and dry
in the sun (see Harvest)
Order spring bulbs
Record vegetable successes
and failures in order to plan
for future years
Sow green manure, such as
hardy red clover or vetch (see
October/Nurturing Your Soil)
Support tomatoes and
pepper plants
Turn your compost heap;
water if it is very dry

SEPTEMBER

SEPTEMBER

SEPTEMBER

OCTOBER

Harvest all vegetables and flowers that might not survive a sudden frost. Start digging over the plot to prepare for next year. October sowings in a mild climate can produce strong and healthy plants. If growing blueberries, plant in acid soil in pairs – different cultivars/similar flowering time – for a really successful crop.

(Left) Winter salad ready for planting out.

(Bottom) Kale leaves sweeten with frost and are harvested as a cut-and-come-again crop.

SOWING OUTDOORS

Legumes Broad beans, mangetout peas
Roots radishes
Salad and leaves Rocket, spinach, and winter lettuces can be sown under cloches

PLANTING OUT

Alliums Garlic, onion sets
Brassicas Cauliflowers, spring cabbages
Fruit Blueberries (plant in pots unless you have acid soil), strawberries, rhubarb
Salad and leaves Winter and spring lettuces

KEEPING THE PLOT

Compost all dying plants (unless diseased)
Cut back asparagus ferns and Jerusalem artichokes
Dig over all empty areas and cover with a compost/manure mix
Draw up soil around stems of brassicas to keep them stable
Earth up celery, leeks
Fork in green manures such as phacelia
Lift all remaining potatoes
Mulch celeriac and parsnips
Plant spring bulbs
Prune blackberries and raspberries
Sweep up leaves and leave them to rot in black bags or cages for one to two years

OCTOBER

OCTOBER

OCTOBER

NURTURING YOUR SOIL

Your compost heap is a priority and should be a balance of green (kitchen waste, grass clippings) and brown (woody cuttings, shredded paper/cardboard). A double compost bin is preferable: one with organic matter ready for use, while the other rots down (see opposite, top left). Covering your compost with an old carpet or piece of wood keeps in the warmth and speeds up rotting. Turning your compost once or twice a year improves results. Burn any diseased material.

If there are trees nearby, sweep autumn leaves into a cage or store when damp in black plastic rubbish bags to create leaf mould.

(Left) Green manure, such as phacelia, crimson clover or buckwheat, prevents soil erosion and when dug in returns nutrients to the soil.

(Far right) Pack comfrey leaves into a bucket or large saucepan, cover and leave for six weeks. Drain off the liquid fertilizer and dilute 15:1 with water to feed your plants.

(Below) An incinerator is useful for burning weeds and diseased plants (and baking potatoes). Always check your allotments' regulations before lighting fires.

NOVEMBER

Dig over your plot before it gets too cold and spread a thick layer of well-rotted organic matter over it, giving the worms time to work it into the soil over the winter. If you have a bonfire, check your allotments' regulations and always light with consideration to others.

(Opposite, left) Cure squashes in the sun before storing.

(Below) Broad beans, started indoors will be ready for planting out.

SOWING OUTDOORS

Legumes Broad beans and peas can still be sown but protect from mice and pigeons
Salad and leaves Spinach, lettuce

PLANTING OUTSIDE

Alliums Garlic, onion sets
Fruit and rhubarb All currants, blackberries, blueberries (need acid soil), gooseberries, raspberries, and rhubarb
Legumes Broad beans and peas if sown indoors earlier in pots. Remember to net well.

KEEPING THE PLOT

Beware of hungry mice and rats and protect your crops
Clean and tie all bamboo canes and stakes into bundles
Cover dahlia tubers with a protective layer of straw or mulch; alternatively dig up and store in dry compost until the spring
Cut down globe artichokes and protect crowns with mulch or straw
Dig in green manure sown in late summer
Dig over your plot and add plenty of well-rotted organic matter
Lift carrots, beetroot, Jerusalem artichokes and store. Parsnips can stay in the ground.
Net over-wintering brassicas; trim any yellow leaves
Prepare a new asparagus bed for planting up in the spring
Protect cauliflower heads from frost by covering with outside leaves
Prune gooseberry and currant bushes
Remove all finished annuals and vegetable plants
Sweep up leaves and leave them to rot in black bags or cages for one to two years
Wood chippings are useful for spreading along muddy paths

NOVEMBER

NOVEMBER

NOVEMBER

DECEMBER

With most vegetables over, December is when you forgive brassicas for being slow growing and greedy for space. Brussels sprouts, kale and some root crops, such as parsnips, actually benefit from frost. Celeriac takes a light frost but lift it before any extreme cold. Now is your last chance to dig and tidy the plot this year.

KEEPING THE PLOT

Clear any dead plants from your plot

Clean flower pots, seed trays and tools

Draw up soil around leggy Brussels sprouts to keep them stable or stake them

Order seeds for next year

Prune currant bushes

Remove yellow leaves from salad leaves and brassicas

Spread well-rotted manure or compost on your plot if you have not already done so

Start planning your plot for next year with crop rotation in mind (see Crop Rotation)

Tidy your shed or storage chest. Check that they are weatherproof and secure.

(Below) Kale is ornamental and very hardy. Grow a selection of varieties to pick as cut-and-come-again crops throughout the winter.

(Below, left) Raised beds are ready for planting up in the coming year. The hardy green manure in the foreground will be dug straight into the soil in the spring.

SOWING AND PLANTING OUTDOORS

Fruit and rhubarb
Plant blackberries, currants, gooseberries, raspberries and rhubarb
Legumes It is still not too late to sow broad beans and peas in mild climates or plant out if sown earlier in pots,
but protect with strong netting
Salad and leaves
Winter lettuce and rocket make good mid-winter crops and should still germinate

DECEMBER

DECEMBER

DECEMBER

ENCOURAGING ALLIES

Remember there are others constantly working on your behalf in your plot. As nearly one-third of what we eat depends on pollination, bees and butterflies are essential allies. Some allotments have beehives (left). Sow green manure such as phacelia and you will not only improve your soil/allotment's fertility but have a plot full of bees. Woodlice and worms help break down the contents of your compost heap, while earthworms draw down any organic matter you have spread on the soil, saving you from having to dig it in. Ladybirds and lacewings devour aphids; a hedgehog's diet includes slugs and caterpillars. If you use pesticides, spray at night or early morning when pollinators are inactive.

(Opposite page, far right) Use hollow canes such as bamboo, seed heads and twigs to create a 'bug hotel'.

(Opposite page, centre) Even a small amount of water encourages frogs and toads, and provides an important water source for birds.

(Left) Hedgehogs like dry spots such as wood piles for hibernation.

Encourage insects by planting buddleia, artichokes (below), echinacea, verbena, lavender and sunflowers. All are magnets for bees and butterflies. Sunflower heads left on the ground provide seeds for birds (bottom, left).

CROP ROTATION

The idea of crop rotation is to avoid growing the same crop, or type of crop, in the same place over subsequent years. Crops that are grown in the same place year after year suffer from a build-up in the soil of their own specific pests and diseases. Such pests and diseases are often able to over-winter in the soil and get a head start in the spring if their favourite food

(your crop) is planted just where they emerge. To avoid this, you could just alternate crops, one year on and one year off – in the same place, but it is better to give the pests and diseases a little longer to die off.

Grouping crops also means that you can apply soil treatments specific to the requirements of each crop to

the whole bed, such as well-rotted manure for legumes and lime for brassicas, rather than having to treat small individual areas.

The qualities and growth habits of each crop can be used to the advantage of the following crop, and so it can pay to bear these in mind when choosing an order for your rotation.

The four main groups are:

Alliums onions, garlic, leeks and shallots

Brassicas including Brussels sprouts, cauliflower, kale, kohl rabi, cabbages and broccoli

Legumes Peas and beans

Roots and tubers including aubergines, peppers, potatoes, tomatoes, celeriac, carrots, celery, parsley and parsnips

In practice alliums are often grouped with legumes, as suggested in the three-year cycle below. You will notice that some commonly grown crops, such as pumpkins, courgettes and salad crops, are not included in this list. This is mainly because they do not have too many problems and can be fitted in wherever you have space among the other crops. As a precaution, however, it would be wise to avoid planting them in the same spot every year.

Each column below represents your plot, subdivided into three plant groups, in a given year. The location of these groups is rotated in a three-year cycle with miscellaneous crops filtered in where possible to maximize seasonal planting.

YEAR 1

Legumes

Brassicas

Roots and tubers

YEAR 2

Brassicas

Roots and tubers

Legumes

YEAR 3

Roots and tubers

Legumes

Brassicas

YEAR 1

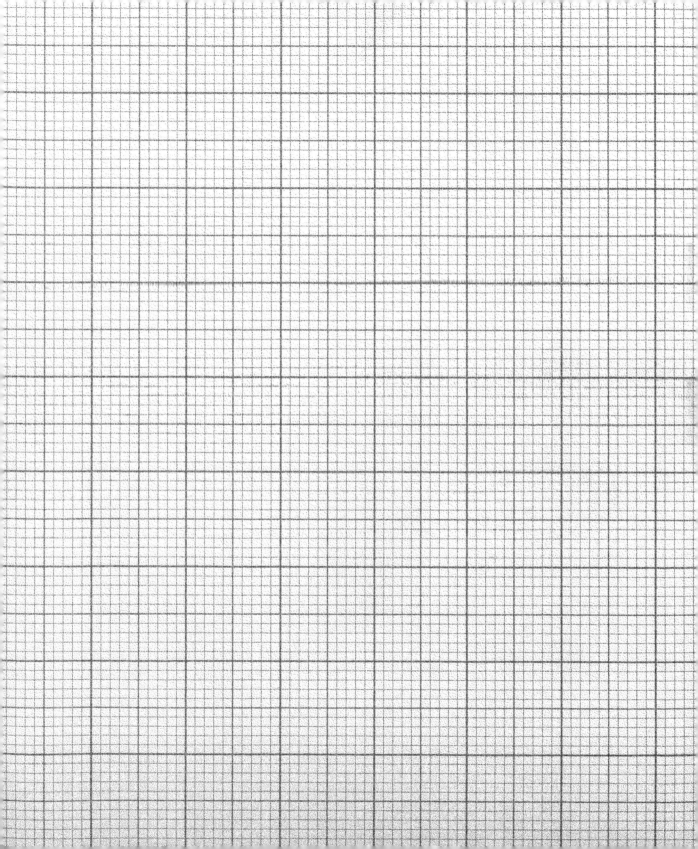

YEAR 2

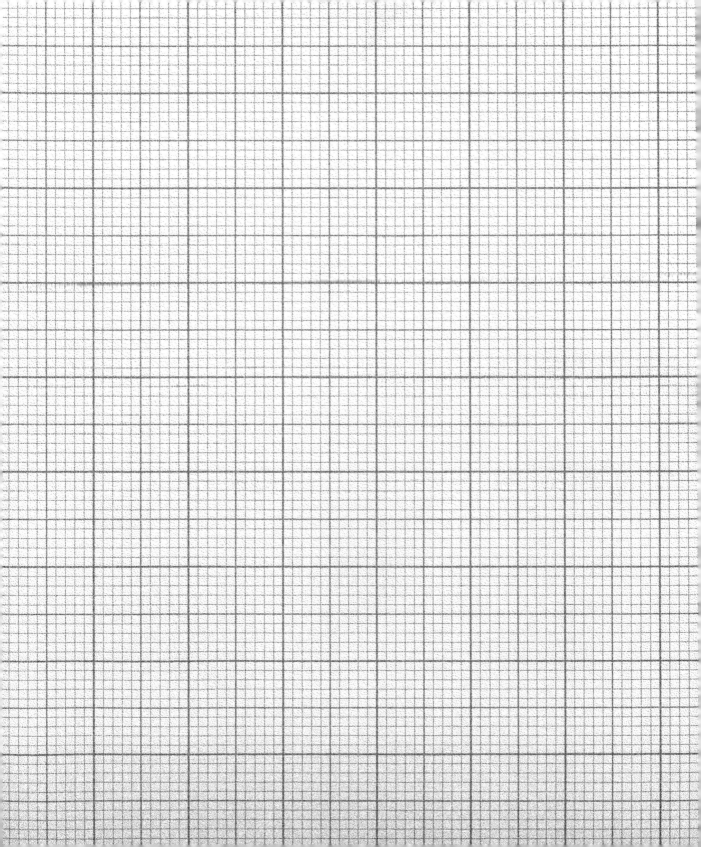

YEAR 3

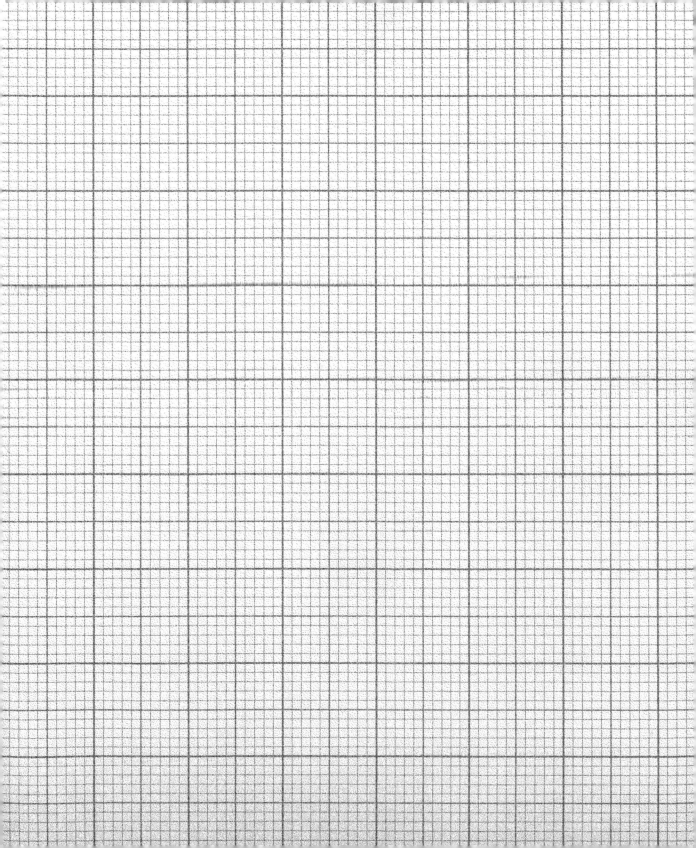

NOTES

NOTES

NOTES

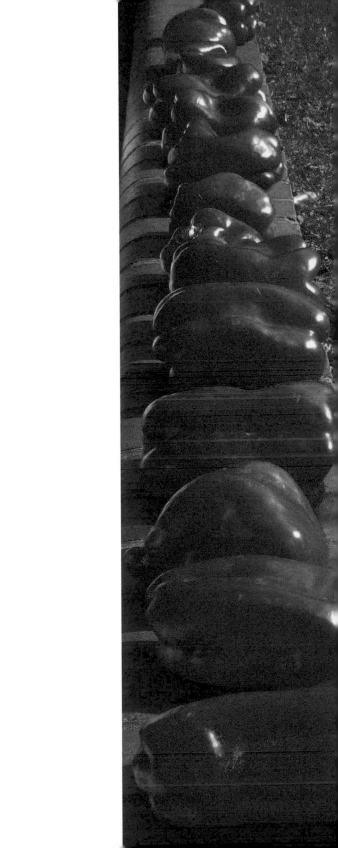

NOTES

CONTACTS

SUPPLIERS

Name:	Name:
Tel:	Tel:
Address:	Address:
Email:	Email:
Name:	Name:
Tel:	Tel:
Address:	Address:
Email:	Email:
Name:	Name:
Tel:	Tel:
Address:	Address:
Email:	Email:
Name:	Name:
Tel:	Tel:
Address:	Address:
Email:	Email:

Name:	Name:
Tel:	Tel:
Address:	Address:
Email:	Email:
Name:	Name:
Tel:	Tel:
Address:	Address:
Email:	Email:
Name:	Name:
Tel:	Tel:
Address:	Address:
Email:	Email:
Name:	Name:
Tel:	Tel:
Address:	Address:
Email:	Email:

SUPPLIERS

Name:	Name:
Tel:	Tel:
Address:	Address:
Email:	Email:
Name:	Name:
Tel:	Tel:
Address:	Address:
Email:	Email:
Name:	Name:
Tel:	Tel:
Address:	Address:
Email:	Email:
Name:	Name:
Tel:	Tel:
Address:	Address:
Email:	Email: